# 1993–2005

# INDEX

Published by
Boston Common Press Limited Partnership
17 Station Street
Brookline, Massachusetts 02445

ISBN: 0-936184-84-1, $12.95
ISSN: 1068-2821

To get home delivery of future issues of *Cook's Illustrated*
magazine, call 1-800-526-8442 or write to the above address.

Key: **BC** = Back Cover

# A

1993–2005

BUTTERMILK/
CAKES

**Buttermilk** *(cont.)*
Mashed Potatoes . . . Nov/Dec 05 24
Ranch . . . Nov/Dec 05 24
microwaving to room temperature . . Sep/Oct 04 30
Pecan Pie with Raisins . . . Nov/Dec 95 8
powdered vs. "real" . . . Mar/Apr 02 2–3
science of . . . Jul/Aug 93 1
substitutes for . . . May/Jun 05 16
Sweet Curry Marinade with . . . Jul/Aug 01 15
Waffles . . . Nov/Dec 93 27–28
**Butternut squash** . . . Nov/Dec 94 15
Braised, with Dried Apricots, Raisins, and Madras Spices . . . Jan/Feb 96 26
dicing . . . Sep/Oct 05 31
field guides . . . Nov/Dec 93 14
. . . Jan/Feb 98 BC
grilling . . . Jul/Aug 96 9
Mashed, with Ginger . . . Nov/Dec 94 15
in minestrone . . . Sep/Oct 98 7
pre-peeled and sliced . . . Sep/Oct 05 14
pureeing for soup . . . May/Jun 02 3
Risotto . . . Sep/Oct 05 14–15
with Spinach and Toasted Pine Nuts . . . Sep/Oct 05 15
Roasted, with Shallots and Thyme . . . Nov/Dec 94 15
Soup . . . Nov/Dec 01 8
Curried, with Cilantro Yogurt . . . Nov/Dec 01 8
with Ginger, Pureed . . . Nov/Dec 96 23
Silky . . . Nov/Dec 01 8
**Butter paddles (butter hands or Scotch hands)** . . . Mar/Apr 03 3
**Butterscotch**
Cookies . . . Nov/Dec 96 20
Cream Pie . . . Mar/Apr 96 24

## C

**Cabbage(s).** *See also* Bok choy; Coleslaw
blanching . . . Jan/Feb 98 4
Braised, with Parsley and Thyme . . . Sep/Oct 96 9
braise-sautéing . . . Sep/Oct 96 9
Chinese . . . Charter Issue 6–7
field guide . . . Mar/Apr 99 BC
growing your own . . . Charter Issue 7
Corned Beef and, New England Style . . Mar/Apr 97 10–11
Cream-Braised, with Lemon and Shallots . . . Sep/Oct 96 9
field guides . . . Mar/Apr 99 BC
. . . Mar/Apr 01 BC
in minestrone . . . Sep/Oct 98 7
napa . . . Charter Issue 6
field guide . . . Mar/Apr 99 BC
Noodle Soup with Chicken and, Vietnamese-Style . . . Mar/Apr 99 20
Seafood Casserole . . . Charter Issue 6
red
discoloration of . . . Jan/Feb 99 9
field guide . . . Mar/Apr 99 BC
Root Vegetables with Rosemary and, Pan-Braised . . . Jan/Feb 96 26
removing leaves from . . . Sep/Oct 95 4
Risotto with Country Ham and . . . Mar/Apr 94 19
salads. *See also* Coleslaw
with Apple and Fennel, Sweet and Sour . . . Sep/Oct 99 18
Confetti, with Spicy Peanut Dressing . . . Sep/Oct 99 18
Red Pepper and, with Lime-Cumin Vinaigrette . . . Sep/Oct 99 18
Seafood Casserole . . . Charter Issue 6
shredded and cleaned, storing . . . May/Jun 00 2
slicing . . . Jul/Aug 94 16
Stir-Fried . . . Charter Issue 7
and Bean Sprouts with Cilantro and Lime . . . Jan/Feb 99 11
stuffed, wilting cabbage leaves for . . . May/Jun 97 3
**Cabrales** . . . May/Jun 99 15
field guide . . . Jan/Feb 02 BC
sources for . . . May/Jun 99 32
**Cacciatore, Chicken** . . . Sep/Oct 00 18–19
**Cacciatorini, field guide** . . . Sep/Oct 04 BC
**Cactus pear, preparing** . . . Jan/Feb 94 17
**Caesar**
Dressing . . . May/Jun 02 13
Tofu . . . Sep/Oct 97 23
Salad . . . Sep/Oct 97 23
Chicken . . . May/Jun 02 12–13
**"Caesar" Dip with Parmesan and Anchovies** . . . Sep/Oct 02 13
***Café Cook Book, The*** **(Gray and Rogers)** . . . Nov/Dec 00 31
**Café Royale spoons** . . . Nov/Dec 98 3
***Café Spice Namaste*** **(Todiwala)** . . . Nov/Dec 00 31
**Caffè Latte** . . . Sep/Oct 93 28
Granita . . . May/Jun 94 25
**Caffè Mocha** . . . Sep/Oct 93 28
**Cajun (cuisine)**
Chicken and Shrimp Jambalaya . . . May/Jun 02 10–11
Spice Rub . . . Jul/Aug 02 20
**Cake carriers, lining with nonskid shelf liners** . . . Sep/Oct 04 5
**Cake cutters, rating of** . . . Jan/Feb 05 32
**Cake flour.** *See* Flour(s)—cake
**Cake mixers or cake whisks, English** . . . Nov/Dec 93 3
sources for . . . Nov/Dec 93 32
**Cake pans.** *See also* Bundt pans; Tube pan(s)
baking more than one at a time . . . Sep/Oct 03 17
best . . . Sep/Oct 03 17
combining greasing and flouring of . . . Nov/Dec 01 5
depth of . . . Mar/Apr 00 3
dusting with cocoa powder . . . Nov/Dec 98 2
flipping with dish towel . . . Jan/Feb 01 17
greasing and flouring . . . Sep/Oct 03 17
lining with parchment paper . . . Mar/Apr 99 4
. . . Jan/Feb 02 17
. . . Sep/Oct 03 16
nonstick, sources for . . . May/Jun 02 32
ratings of . . . Nov/Dec 99 28–29
. . . Mar/Apr 00 3
. . . Jan/Feb 05 25
rotating with tongs . . . Jan/Feb 01 16
size substitutions and . . . Sep/Oct 03 31
sources for . . . Nov/Dec 99 32
. . . May/Jun 00 32
. . . May/Jun 02 32
. . . Sep/Oct 03 32
. . . Jan/Feb 05 32
square, sources for . . . May/Jun 00 32
**Cake plates**
keeping clean while frosting cake . . . May/Jun 97 4
. . . Jan/Feb 02 17
lining with parchment paper . . . Mar/Apr 99 4
**Cake platters, makeshift** . . . Jul/Aug 99 5
**Cake rounds, cardboard, sources for** . . Mar/Apr 00 32
**Cakes.** *See also* Cheesecakes; Chocolate(s)—cakes; Coffee cake(s); Frostings; Pound Cake
Almond Meringue, with Strawberry and Vanilla Ice Cream . . . May/Jun 95 13
Angel Food . . . Charter Issue 10–12
cake pans for . . . Charter Issue 12
cutting . . . Nov/Dec 96 2
whipping egg whites for . . . Sep/Oct 99 17
Apple . . . Sep/Oct 01 22–23
birthday, all-purpose . . . May/Jun 95 18–19
Blackberry Jam . . . Sep/Oct 98 23
Blueberry Buckle . . . Jul/Aug 05 22–23
Bundt
Apple . . . Sep/Oct 01 23
Chocolate Sour Cream . . . Jan/Feb 04 22–23
ensuring easy release from pan . . . Jan/Feb 03 23
removing from pan . . . Nov/Dec 96 5
Carrot . . . Jan/Feb 98 22–23
. . . Mar/Apr 03 24–25
alternative mixing methods for . Nov/Dec 03 32
with Cream Cheese Frosting . . . Mar/Apr 03 25
oil vs. butter in . . . Jan/Feb 98 23
**Cakes** *(cont.)*
with Pineapple and Pecans . . . Jan/Feb 98 23
with Raisins and Walnuts . . . Jan/Feb 98 23
Spiced, with Vanilla Bean–Cream Cheese Frosting . . . Mar/Apr 03 25
with Tangy Cream Cheese Frosting . . . Jan/Feb 98 23
Chiffon (with variations) . . . May/Jun 96 6–8
tube pans for . . . May/Jun 96 32
coconut
Granny's Speckled . . . Mar/Apr 94 21
Layer . . . Mar/Apr 01 24–25
Lemon Chiffon . . . May/Jun 96 8
covers for . . . May/Jun 00 5
cupcakes
baking without muffin tin . . . Jan/Feb 03 24
Dark Chocolate . . . Mar/Apr 05 24–25
decorating . . . Nov/Dec 03 5
protecting for safe transport . . . May/Jun 03 4
wrapping neatly . . . May/Jun 04 5
Yellow, with Chocolate Ganache Frosting . . . Jan/Feb 03 24–25
decorating . . . Jul/Aug 94 23
. . . May/Jun 95 16–17
. . . Nov/Dec 03 5
basket weave . . . May/Jun 95 17
borders . . . May/Jun 95 17
chocolate decorations, simple . . . Mar/Apr 96 16
flourless chocolate . . . Nov/Dec 98 5
fork designs . . . Mar/Apr 00 17
frosting swirls . . . Mar/Apr 99 5
garnishing sides . . . Jan/Feb 99 5
make-ahead chocolate shapes for . . Jul/Aug 97 4
with nuts . . . Mar/Apr 00 17
powdered sugar and cocoa designs . . . Mar/Apr 00 17
removing stencils from tops . . . Mar/Apr 99 5
rosettes and stars . . . May/Jun 95 17
side swags . . . May/Jun 95 16
silky look in . . . Jul/Aug 95 4
tool sources for . . . Jul/Aug 94 32
. . . May/Jun 95 32
writing . . . May/Jun 95 17
fillings for
Coconut-Pecan . . . Jul/Aug 94 25
Espresso-Mascarpone Cream . . . Nov/Dec 00 25
keeping from bleeding into frosting . . . Mar/Apr 95 4
Lemon, Rich . . . Sep/Oct 98 23
Raspberry-Almond . . . May/Jun 95 19
Raspberry Mousse . . . Jan/Feb 94 14
flour for . . . Mar/Apr 96 3
Genoise . . . Nov/Dec 95 10–11
Grand Marnier, with Neoclassic Orange Buttercream . . . Nov/Dec 95 11
Gingerbread, Old-Fashioned . . . Nov/Dec 95 22–23
Apple Upside-Down . . . Nov/Dec 95 23
with Dried Fruit . . . Nov/Dec 95 23
Orange Sauce for . . . Nov/Dec 95 23
Grand Marnier, with Neoclassic Orange Buttercream . . . Nov/Dec 95 11
homemade mixes for . . . Jan/Feb 00 4
layer
Chocolate, with Chocolate Cream Frosting, Old-Fashioned . . . Jul/Aug 94 24
Chocolate, with Meringue Frosting, Reduced-Guilt . . . Jul/Aug 94 25
Coconut . . . Mar/Apr 01 24–25
Coconut, Granny's Speckled . . . Mar/Apr 94 21
correcting uneven layers for . . . Jan/Feb 05 17
Devil's Food, Moist and Tender . . Mar/Apr 00 24–25
Devil's Food, Velvet, with Coffee Buttercream Frosting . . . Jul/Aug 94 24
Devil's Food, with Whipped Cream, Classic . . . Jul/Aug 94 24
frosting . . . Jan/Feb 98 22
. . . Mar/Apr 99 24

**1993–2005**